MADE TO ORDER

CAMPION PLATT
MADE TO ORDER

WRITTEN WITH MARC KRISTAL

THE MONACELLI PRESS

Copyright © 2010 The Monacelli Press, a division of Random House, Inc., and Campion Platt.

All rights reserved. Published in the United States by The Monacelli Press,
a division of Random House, Inc., New York.

The Monacelli Press and the M design are registered trademarks of Random House, Inc.

Library of Congress Cataloging-in-Publication Data

Platt, Campion.
Made to order / by Campion Platt ; foreword by Jay McInerney. — 1st ed.
p. cm.
ISBN 978-1-58093-280-6 (hardcover)
1. Platt, Campion. 2. Interior architecture--United States--History--21st century.
3. Interior decoration--United States--History--21st century. I. Title.
NA737.P475A4 2010
729.092--dc22   2010010899

Printed in China

10 9 8 7 6 5 4 3 2 1
First edition

www.monacellipress.com

Design by Think Studio, NYC

CONTENTS

FOREWORD BY JAY MCINERNEY   6

INTRODUCTION   8

TELLING A STORY

TROPICAL MISCHIEF   14

JEWEL BOX   32

CAPTAIN'S HOUSE   42

HEAVEN'S CHAMBER   54

OPEN SPACES

WHITE LOFT   64

MODERN RESTORATION   76

MANHATTAN HOUSE   82

APARTMENT LIVING

FIFTH AVENUE ART HOUSE   96

MURRAY HILL TOWNHOUSE   106

CONTRASTS

HUDSON VALLEY PASTORAL   120

CARNEGIE HILL ZEN   134

HIGHRISE REDUX   146

NATURE AND CRAFT

SKY LOUNGE   158

COUNTRY MANOR   168

CITY HUES   182

TRIBECA LOFT   196

SOLUTIONS

ASTOR PLACE   210

WRITER'S RETREAT   220

ACKNOWLEDGMENTS   230

PHOTOGRAPHY CREDITS   232

FOREWORD JAY McINERNEY

Although I have been fortunate enough to have worked with Campion Platt on four different residential projects over the past twenty years I find myself suffering from a form of real estate envy as I peruse this volume. Call it design envy. I want that study/cigar room in Palm Beach. I want to climb that elegantly curved staircase with the gnarled wood railing in Southampton. No, wait, actually what I really want is to entertain my friends in that Art Deco living room on Central Park West. Actually, I'd like to live in most of these rooms. At any rate, it's great to be able to visit them in these pages. Flipping through them reminds me that I've learned quite a bit about design and architecture while observing the growth and development of Campion's ideas and his career. I like to think of Campion's mature aesthetic as modernism with soul.

We'd been friends for several years before I asked Campion to help me combine my apartment with a second apartment that I had purchased directly beneath me in anticipation of the arrival of twins. I had always admired Campion's sense of style, his personal aesthetic, but in this case the challenge involved a knotty engineering and structural problem, not to mention potentially crippling budget constraints. Campion's solution was elegant as well as practical and in the end the finished space seemed to have been waiting all along to manifest itself, though in fact it was wrestled into existence.

When divorce necessitated a move from that particular New York apartment I turned to Campion again to design my bachelor digs. I'm still in awe of the way he transformed a one-bedroom, prewar New York apartment into a beautiful, multipurpose living space. Since the apartment was a rental we weren't able to reconfigure it. Not the least of the challenges I posed for him was the need to accommodate some two thousand volumes of my library, while also leaving me enough wall space to hang my art. In one particularly crafty solution, he designed a room divider to create a discrete office space with a built-in desk and further bookshelf space above.

Once Campion had seized on the theme of writer's retreat, he carried it through the apartment, going so far as to create, in collaboration with a painter, a finish that mimicked sheets of parchment for the walls of the bedroom. I discovered that Campion was almost obsessively concerned with fabrics and finishes, which resulted in a very visually rich environment. Early on we decided on a relatively muted palette of browns, tans, and taupes with black accents. When an early visitor remarked that the color scheme was masculine, Campion responded, "So is my client." Which I thought was a very good answer. (Anyone who wonders about Campion's ability to get in touch with his feminine palette should check out the bedroom suite he designed for his wife in their Soho loft.)

In my little Greenwich Village writer's retreat, he also created a number of custom pieces of furniture that made the most of the limited space. Knowing that I like to entertain he reimagined my sixteen-foot-long foyer as a dining space, and designed a table that seated twelve when needed but folded into a narrow console after the guests went home.

My latest venture with Campion could hardly be more of a departure from our urban design projects. With my wife, Anne, I'd purchased two acres of beachfront property on Ambergris Cay in the Turks and Caicos Islands. We had a vague picture in our minds of a simple Caribbean beach house, a three-bedroom retreat, which Campion fleshed out with a modular design that involves three separate pavilions around a central courtyard—a master bedroom, a great room, and a two-bedroom house. The courtyard was in part a solution to the problem of strong northeast winter trade winds. Since there's hardly any rain on the island the open plan between the pavilions seemed ideal and afforded many views from each room. Although Campion is a modernist, he chose in this case something closer to the local vernacular—something, in fact, which bodied forth our fantasy of a tropical beach house.

The beach house was conceived as the guest house to a larger five-bedroom domicile, which we hope will rise on the bluff above it someday. This house was also built around a central courtyard with two bedroom wings framing the open space. We spent many hours with Campion designing this particular house, walking the lot, placing rooms, and getting lifted 15 feet above the bluff in a cherry picker in order to assess the view from the future second-floor balcony. The resulting house, which includes a turret facing the sea, so far exists only on paper, although I have no doubt that Campion can visualize it much more clearly than I can. With luck it will become a reality in the near future. In the meantime I will be thumbing through the following pages, looking for ideas and envying his other clients.

INTRODUCTION

If you've landed on this page, it might be by mistake.

I know that may sound funny. I also know that because I'm no different from anyone who picks up a design book: the first thing (sometimes the only thing) I want to do is look at the photographs. But if you don't read the text, you might be misled by what you're seeing.

Rather than discovering a "signature style," you'll find homes that appear to be quite different from one another—sleek modern lofts, an early twentieth-century manor, an old sea captain's house, urbane apartments. What's more, these residences—many of which are luxurious, glamorous, and have been published in high-end design magazines—may seem beyond most people's reach, with lessons not applicable to everyday life.

If you read the accompanying descriptions, however, you'll soon discover a common thread: each of these residences evolved from a few simple ideas—a story, if you will—which came out of conversations with my clients (or, in some cases, friends and family) about their dreams and aspirations. And you'll find that the same process can succeed for anyone, at any budget, working with or without a design professional.

That's because the ideas that form the building blocks of a successful project—like every aspect of the design process—are worthy of close consideration. And the best way to consider things, I've found, is to make them to order.

In fact, the impulse toward customization—creating or seeking out things that are unique expressions of one's own personality and approach—is an essential part of human nature. When we're young, we distinguish ourselves through sports, or by playing music, or with our hobbies and collections. We delight in our first made-to-order birthday cake, and even if a woman's never had anything specially created for her, she'll find someone to design her wedding dress. The bespoke influence has even crept into mass-market products—you can get special sizes from Levi's, unique colors from Nike, custom-made boots from Timberland, and create your own iPod playlist. Why should your home be any less personalized?

In the projects that follow, you'll find many things that are made to order—one of the most important being the actual process. Rule number one, in my view, is that handcrafting a home of one's own should be a pleasure, not a chore or something you turn over to "the experts" without comment. That doesn't mean there won't be miscues, wrong turns and moments of indecision. But as we all know, a lot of things that seem scary are actually fun—indeed, the scary part is the fun part—and design is no different. And the unexpected discoveries, the creative collaborations, and most of all the chance to put your personal stamp on every room are what make your home your own.

Although my projects tend toward the contemporary, I've found that clients appreciate the tactile quality inherent in craftsmanship—especially in contrast to the metropolitan experience, in which everything is so hard-edged—and so much of my interior and furniture design work is bespoke as well. While I don't build things personally, I remain very interested in how things are put together, and spend a great deal of time watching craftspeople set their tools to wood, stone, and metal. This enables me not only to respect the true nature of the material, but to understand how far I can push the design envelope.

And though it may not seem so, making things to order is also socially responsible. In this regard, the question of provenance—typically applied to valuable objects and antiques, to help establish their legitimacy—remains as important as the source of food is to a gourmet. From where does a chair or a fabric come? Was it produced by a local maker using sustainable materials—and if not, how far did it travel and how much fuel did the trip require? In a way, this represents an enlightened return to the period prior to the Industrial Revolution, when virtually everything was custom crafted. Making things to order, once again, is becoming the norm—and, in the process, connecting us to our humanity.

Don't get me wrong—I do hope you'll look at the pictures, and enjoy what you see. But I hope as well that what follows will provide you with a design tool kit of sorts, and serve as an inspiration. Many of my colleagues teach, and while my business makes that impossible right now, this is my way of sharing the knowledge gained from twenty-five years of experience, and of demonstrating that the design process is a fun one in which everyone can participate.

In other words, this book isn't for my fellow designers. It's been made to order—for you.

TELLING A **STORY**

Everyone has had the experience of telling a story, whether to a child at bedtime or to a bunch of friends over a glass of wine, or in some other context. But what might it mean to "tell a story" with architecture?

Here's an example: A few years ago, I was asked by a Venezuelan couple to design their pied-à-terre in Manhattan. The apartment they had chosen posed a range of challenges, and I was at a loss as to how best to resolve them. While I was wrestling with the project, I went on a meditation retreat to Asia, and in the middle of it—remembering that my clients lived most of the year in the tropics—I had a vision of the pied-à-terre as a South American courtyard house: a place with an open-air entry garden, from which all of the home's rooms and circulation paths would unfold. Typically, I develop concepts through a give-and-take with the architects and designers in my office, after devising a program with a client. This time, captivated by my theme, I sat down with a sketchbook and drew the entire apartment—from the broad organizational strokes to the rooms and the ways they communicated to the architectural details and furnishings—in a matter of days.

The tale, as you will see in the coming pages, might also be about the lair of an old sea captain or inspired by a bunch of upper-crust Brits in colonial Africa. But whatever the case, my experience drove home one of the most valuable things I've learned: every successful project grows out of a story—and I can't begin until I have found the story I want to tell.

This lesson, I should add, is not only of use to design professionals. Finding a story becomes especially important when you consider that 80 percent of home furnishings are purchased not by designers, but by people shopping for their own dwellings. I can't count the number of times I've been asked to help out clients who had bought very beautiful, very costly vintage pieces by world-famous names—and wondered why nothing seemed to go together. The reason was that no unifying idea guided the design approach to their purchases.

Whether you're a homeowner or a professional, finding a compelling story—or, if you prefer, a theme or concept—enables you to consider every decision with what amounts to a dependable true/false meter. At the largest scale, defining your inspiration helps to establish architectural principles that will organize the design—a courtyard house, for example, has certain signature elements upon which to draw. But having a story also helps with the details. Is this chair, wall covering, or rug contributing to the tale I want to tell? Or does it somehow strike a wrong note even though it's beautiful or "important"? If you have developed a strong concept, you will make fewer mistakes, create interiors that are more original, imaginative, and authentically your own—and you will be practicing the craft of interior design rather than simply decorating.

Of course, the prospect of coming up with something that will drive all of a project's design decisions can be daunting. The flip side of the equation is that every space has a story to tell—and so finding a story, at least in part, involves discovering what your home wants to be. If you're at a loss, try jump-starting the process by taking your cues from the architecture. Once you've got a dialogue going, everything that flows from it will be functional, beautiful, and welcoming.

Having said all this, let me add a caveat: if your theme just does not seem to be working after a few tries, don't be afraid to move on. There's a Buddhist saying: "The only way out is in." Immerse yourself in the process—and you will come out with the right story to tell.

TROPICAL MISCHIEF

Grand and elegant Gatsbyesque estates, with beachfront acreage, ballrooms, and bedrooms by the dozen come to mind when we hear the words Palm Beach—hardly houses at all. But like the rest of southern Florida, the city has a simpler side, one that's about the laid-back pleasures of abundant sunshine, fragrant vegetation, and the soothing effects of the sea. That's what my wife Tatiana and I were after when we discovered a 1924 British Colonial Revival house and made it our winter retreat. And just as we didn't want opulence and formality, neither were we interested in the traditional local decorative style, characterized by white-painted wicker and layers of chintz. For me, the task involved adapting the approach I'd developed on my urban projects—favoring strong contrasts, streamlined details, and unfussy layouts—to a tropical house in a very different sort of environment.

We found our story in *White Mischief*, a guilty pleasure of a movie about upper-crust Brits misbehaving in 1940s Kenya. Tatiana and I appreciated the film's hothouse air, the colonial interiors that combined propriety and primitivism. Taking the film's decadence as a departure point, I imported exotic style from Africa to the tropics, then brought it into the present—going native, but with design sophistication.

I began by securing landmark status for the exterior to ensure that regardless of who owns it, the house's history remains intact. Then we opened up the ground-floor plan: removing walls, enlarging doors and surrounding them with oversize custom frames, creating views from the entry gallery through the living room to the spaces beyond. The interior design scheme established a base of multiple contrasts—dark against light, pattern versus color—on which I built layers of detail that both established the house's style and personalized it. Some of these, such as the nailhead furnishings and objects upholstered in faux python skin and raffia, referenced the film directly. Others—the bust of a mythical goddess encrusted with seashells in the entry, the library's pickled cypress walls—put a Palm Beach spin on the British Colonial sensibility. And there is a strong contemporary influence to be found in everything from the artworks to the extensive use of Lucite to the reflective lacquer and polished stone finishes.

For our efforts, the city of Palm Beach bestowed the Polly Earl Award on the historic house and its interiors, of which we were very proud. Ultimately, it must be admitted, Tatiana and I wandered afield of our cinematic inspiration. But it provided just the right beginning, one that enabled us to construct a strong, personal narrative—and we still occasionally screen *White Mischief* on the theater-size screen overlooking the pool.

The Garden Book

DAVID MORRIS

PAUL KLEE THE NATURE OF CREATION Hayward Gallery

FURNITURE OF THE DUTCH PERIOD IN CEYLON

The Vertical Garden   PATRICK BLANC

Both the cabana room, above, and a casual dining area, right, share a color connection and open onto the pool area. The wood-grain tile floor in the dining room also relates in color to the adjacent kitchen, creating visual continuity between the spaces. The white lacquer table was custom-designed to match the vintage chairs.

floating crown
blush pink walls
large art wall
palanquin side board

room divider
cove light
full mirror
stone top

sta cabinets
floating base
bifolding rattan door
green camouflage stone top
green cushions

tribe table

Removing a wall between the living and dining areas opened up the ground floor's public rooms to create a loftlike space; a white lacquer cabinet quietly divides the two zones.

In one guest room, above, inspiration for the lofted bed frame derived from the necessity of building it over the stairway; the walls are covered in light-brown raffia. In another, opposite, a predominantly blue color scheme extends even to the artwork.

Placing the shower behind the movie wall and inserting a pool, Jacuzzi, daybed, and two benches in the residual space helped to maximize the functionality of this tightly confined pool area.

Each of the living room's furniture pieces was custom-designed with an eye toward contrasting warm tones and luxurious materials with strongly architectural elements. The latter is embodied by the four-piece butcher-block coffee table. Throughout, large-scale furnishings help the rooms appear larger and the ceiling higher.

The cloudy maple wall that begins in the living room flows into the dining room/lounge, left, uniting the two spaces in mood despite their distance from each other in this pied-à-terre. A warm-toned, gun-metal built-in over the walnut bar, above, frames the owners' photo of a Venezuelan mountain range near their primary home.

In the living room, a custom-designed sofa covered in a cashmere—chosen for its comforting texture—amplifies the enveloping warmth of the cloudy maple wall behind.

Custom-designed beds define the character of both the master
suite and the guest room. In the former, above, an overscaled
walnut, burl, and orange velvet bed embraces the room. In the
latter, right, the woven, articulated headboards—accentuated
by braided pillows—give each guest a sense of privacy.

CAPTAIN'S HOUSE

Sited on a history-rich waterside lane in Sag Harbor, a former Long Island whaling village, this small-scale 1857 sea captain's house contrasts pleasantly with the sprawling compounds of nearby East Hampton. When we first began to poke around inside the structure, we discovered a painting, concealed behind a wall, of a bearded, pipe-smoking mariner; I imagined the house as belonging to exactly such a fellow—a man who had gathered an eccentric array of furnishings and objects over decades of global circumnavigation, then retired to live among his treasures. The architectural challenge of maintaining the original charm was complicated, however: an effort of restoration and modernization that preserved the language of the nineteenth century while transforming the small, dark rooms into a relaxed and sunny environment for a young family.

Partly this involved executing a few bold strokes: lifting the structure off its original foundation and inserting a basement with family and guest rooms, and adding a new double-height kitchen wing. More significant was transforming the layout of the first-floor public rooms into a single space. Four fluted wood columns replaced the hallway wall, and the remaining rooms were converted into a loftlike plan loosely divided into living room, den, and dining area. The overall effect is one of delightful openness: entering through the front door, visitors can see all the way through the house to the waterscape beyond.

While I often inject vitality into a design by creating contrasts, respecting this house's historic qualities required that I connect its new elements to the past. Principally this meant establishing relationships between the architecture and furniture through the marriage of details. On the dining room side of the freestanding fireplace, for example, we included a serving buffet with a nineteenth-century-style vertical turnbuckle as part of the fireplace flue, and we replicated it in the understructure of the dining table; conversely, many of the furniture pieces are period antiques, and we migrated some of their beautifully crafted details into the new millwork and custom upholstery. Using a blowtorch, we also flame-finished the wood of the living room coffee tables, an update of the classic craft technique of plunging boards into vats of hot ball bearings. And wherever possible, the design featured rough-and-tumble details that my fantasy sea captain might have fashioned himself, such as the stairway's rope handrails and the "fishhooks" that attach the draperies to their rods.

When we were done, I told my client about the man in the painting, which I'd had framed and hung in the kitchen. She confided that she'd been visited by just such a character in her dreams—and was convinced the place was pleasantly haunted by him.

Handblown glass globes, hand-fitted into a custom chandelier, begin the interior's historic, bespoke feeling that was inspired by the portrait of a sea captain found behind a wall during the house's renovation.

What had once been an enclosed and confining entry hall was replaced with a pair of columns, above, that open a sight-line from the front door through the living and dining rooms and to the water beyond. Simple elements define each zone, such as the freestanding fireplace, right, which floats between the den and dining room, lightly dividing the two spaces.

OPEN SPACES

In New York, what you see out the window is a de facto part of your home.

WHITE LOFT

Our own Soho loft, a promising but unfinished duplex when we first discovered it, presented
all the positives and challenges of open-plan living. The main floor in particular, with its
15-foot-high ceiling and 270-degree views—so important in New York, where what you see
out the window is a de facto part of your home—offered the pleasures of a light-filled,
voluminous expanse of space. At the same time, the loft suffered from the usual drawbacks:
the "shotgun" layout was long, narrow in places, and dark in its nearly windowless center.

I began by laying out the entertaining areas at the front of the first floor. Though it
further narrowed the space, I built out the wall along the entry hallway, to create necessary
storage and a laundry room, concealing it behind lacquered white millwork. Rather than
trying to reduce its presence, I enlarged the living room fireplace into a monumental sculptural
element, adding a secret TV above it and wrapping the entire volume in ebonized
mahogany. Finally, I inserted another element, effectively a box within a box: a diaphanous
kitchen pavilion, also lacquered a gleaming white. Long ago, in architecture school, a professor
taught us that every successful building has three scales, and that is what I created here:
an arrangement of "virtual" rooms that organized the space; the cabinetry and furniture
that defined them; and, not least, the personal accessories, objects and photos that truly
make it our home.

In back, we introduced a slight bend at the end of the hallway leading to the two bedrooms
so that it didn't arrive at an abrupt dead end. Because one of them was overlong, we divided
it in two, producing both a bedroom for my elder son and a cozy yoga room, which has since
become a playroom for my youngest. And a tiny study benefitted from various tricks of the
trade, notably a circular curtain-rail system that, by rounding off and concealing the room's
corners, makes it feel larger than it is. There's also wall-size ebonized cabinetry that makes
a connection to the fireplace in front.

In the original plan, the stair leading to the second floor arrived in the private heart
of the master suite; I reversed it so that, ascending, Tatiana and I come out into the cozy,
light-washed sitting room, facing a wide terrace and magical western view of Soho. With
a ceiling height that's considerably lower than that of the first floor, the emphasis remains
horizontal rather than vertical: we added a low mantelpiece in the sitting area and encircled
the bathroom with pink onyx wainscoting.

About that color: it derived from my desire to create a classically feminine environment
for my wife—but to make pink hip, rather than frilly. With the oranges, yellows, and honey
tones downstairs, the palette reinforces the design's departure from the usual urban-industrial
aesthetic—in favor of something light, ethereal, and gentle.

The difference between architecture and simple
structure is expressed by a semienclosed kitchen
volume, above. By virtue of its lighting and porosity it
seems to float, capsule-like, within the larger room.

Floor-to-ceiling bookshelves in the lounge area of the living room, above, strengthen its connection to the vertical urban landscape outside the windows. Taking the edges out of the den, opposite, by accentuating its curves and softening the corners with curtains draws the space cozily in upon itself.

A master suite that is classically feminine in character yet contemporary in style combines shades of pink with sleek finishes and materials and bold graphics.

Two bedroom suites deal with the loft's 15-foot ceiling heights in separate ways. Wainscotting updated in pink onyx in the master bath, above, emphasizes horizontal lines, while the room at right embraces its strong verticality with floor-to-ceiling curtains.

MODERN RESTORATION

The notion of living and working in the same environment has become more prevalent recently. The owner of this townhouse triplex in Manhattan, however, has been doing it for decades, and in a most original way. Since moving into the apartment in the 1980s, he's opened up his living spaces to his public relations clients to varying degrees while maintaining a separate office for staff, going back and forth between the two as necessary. The result is a home that is "live," "live/work," and "work," with the proportions perpetually in flux.

The problem was that the original layout, cobbled together on the ground and parlor floors of what began as a duplex, wasn't as savvy as its occupant. My client's "meet-and-greet" office occupied the parlor floor, a few steps up from the street, while the ground floor, a few steps below street level, had awkwardly mixed purposes: office in front, private quarters in the rear. Navigating between the two required an up-and-down journey involving two stairways and a route through common areas shared by the building's other occupants. My job was to rationalize the circulation patterns in a way that enabled him to access different areas with greater control and fluency, and to use them more flexibly.

This challenge resulted in the creation of a parlor floor that is effectively a loft: all the spaces—dining room, kitchen, living room, and executive office—can be completely open, communicating with each other when my client is home alone, or selectively closed off with pocket doors during the work day. A single stair descends from this space to a ground-floor hallway, connecting to a four-person office in front and a private master suite in back. And because my client's staff expanded along with his business, we excavated a lower-level office loft that accommodates twelve people in well-appointed comfort.

Appropriately, the apartment's fluid nature is reflected in the design—sometimes it's modern, other times historic, elsewhere a blend of both. We used modern elements and materials, such as the sleek glass-and-metal stair set against the original brick, to establish a clear distinction between old and new architecture. When blending the two was unavoidable, we designed a solution that mediates by subtly lightening and streamlining the craftwork, opening up what had been a series of confining rooms and allowing them to breathe.

The outcome accommodates the flexibility needed for my client's way of life and celebrates open-loft living in a townhouse setting. All of it overlaps and interconnects—public or private as the occasion demands.

A slight separation between the living room and office was achieved through the introduction of a single steel column, left and below, that replaced the preexisting wall and serves as a sculptural object within the space. The combination of historic and contemporary elements produces an open-plan loft space that still expresses the character of an Arts and Crafts townhouse.

The industrial look of the new glass-
and-metal stair, right, is a modern foil
to the rough warmth of the original
brick. Previously confining, the master
bath, opposite, is now well-appointed,
elegantly finished, and spacious.

MANHATTAN HOUSE

Manhattan House, on New York's Upper East Side, captures the special brand of urbane elegance that defined the city in the postwar years. Designed by the American modernist Gordon Bunshaft in 1950, the white-brick apartment complex, which consumes an entire city block, features light-filled residences with panoramic views—pristine spaces that remain ideal for cocktail parties, casual dinners, and the sort of effortlessly refined gatherings that people the world over associate with the magical word "Manhattan."

My design for a two-bedroom apartment in the building reinterpreted that style for our time—while also getting the absolute most from the residence's public space. While gracious, the overall apartment wasn't, in fact, very large. But it featured a 30-by-30-foot living room, and I used a variety of strategies to convert what is normally a room with two functions—living and dining—into a more complex, multifunctional, and inviting set of entertaining spaces.

The first move was to create a dining nook, with a banquette, in the corner by the kitchen, freeing up the circulation space normally required around a dinner table and leaving a larger open plan. To reinforce the formal living room area defined by the fireplace, which projected slightly into the room, we enlarged the fireplace mantel and tucked vertical cove lights behind both sides of it; this allowed the fireplace to "pop" by making the walls on either side of it seem to recess. A 15-foot-long banquette was set against one wall—an unusual element for a residence, but one that established a separate lounge and entertainment area. And we added an extra layer beside the window, in the form of a game table with two chairs. Combined with the open square of floor space beyond the entry foyer, the result was a single room incorporating five distinct subspaces—a room in which to play chess by the window, sip a martini on the banquette, warm oneself by the fire, enjoy a quiet dinner, and welcome arriving guests.

For the fabrics and finishes, I drew inspiration from Grace Kelly, an icon of understated sophistication who had been an early Manhattan House resident. The operative words are reflectivity and pearlescence—glossy walls and floors that blaze with sunlight by day and shimmer after dark, and a sophisticated dove-gray palette with hints of pattern, form, and color. All these elements, along with custom pieces, vintage objects, and artworks, come together to convey a cohesive message—classic postwar style, updated for a new century.

Although sunlit throughout, this oversized 30-by-30-foot living room works best when divided into five distinct areas for sitting, dining, and socializing. Glossy finishes and plush fabrics provide an overlay of urbane elegance.

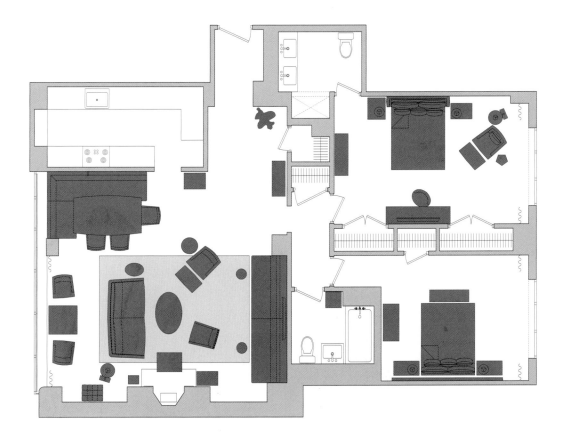

The layering of curtains and Roman shades, right, creates
a simple decorative detail at the window wall, helping to
define a small sitting area established by a game table.

Pillows, upholstered in fabrics from the Campion Platt Metro Cloth collection for Jim Thompson, enliven a banquette, above. At right, a vertical light cove behind the mantelpiece creates the illusion of greater depth.

Moving the dinner table to a nook in one corner of the room opened up options—namely, to add multiple functions to what typically would have been restricted to just a living/dining space.

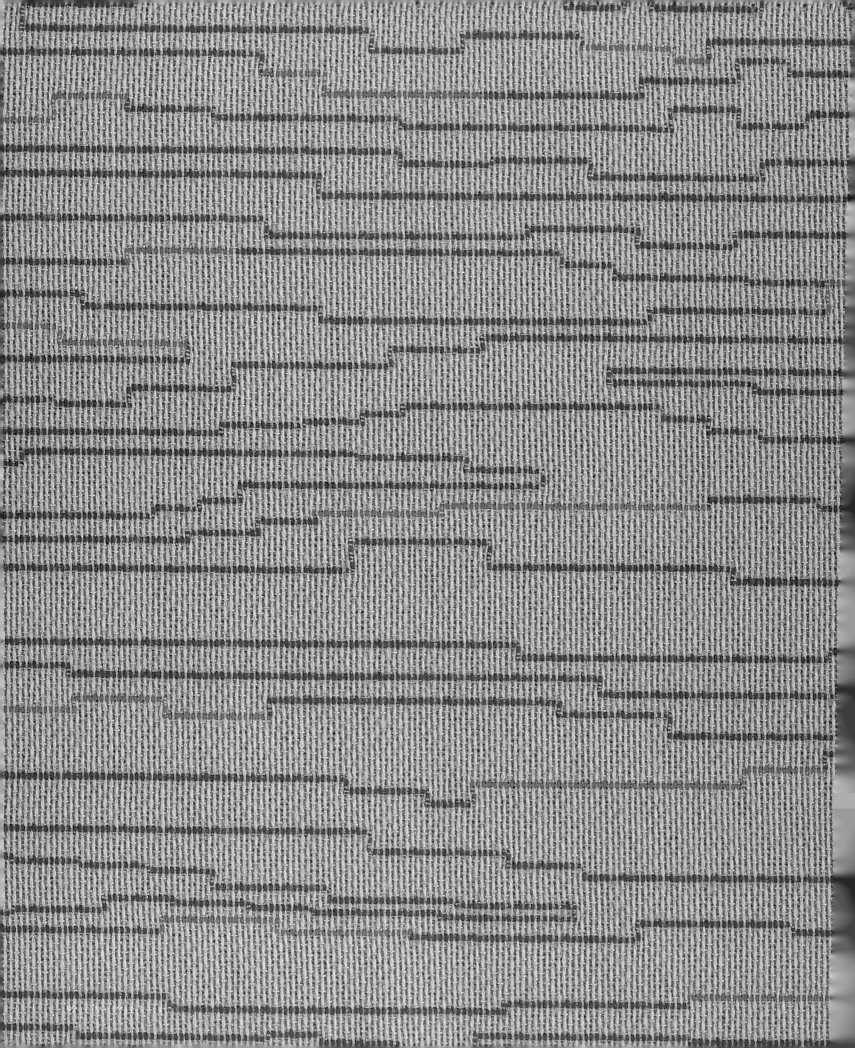

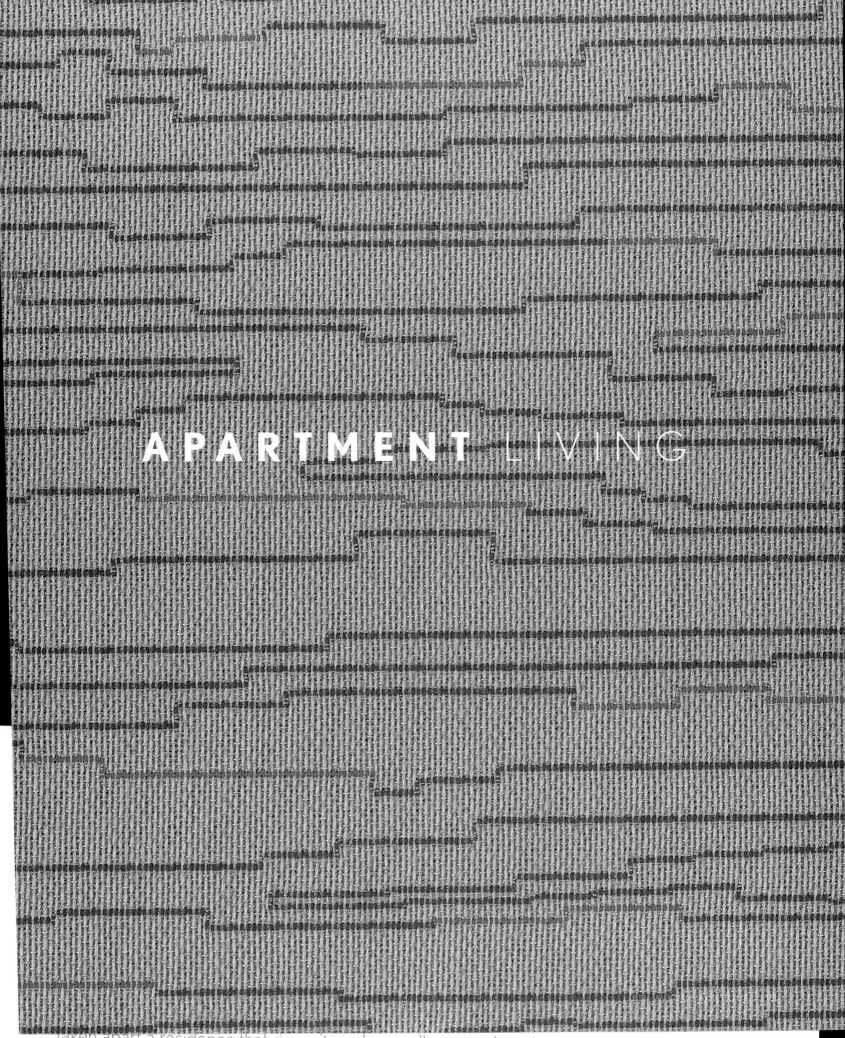

APARTMENT LIVING

taken apart a residence that doesn't work as well as it might, release your preferences into your space and see how they organize themselves. When you put your apartment back together again, you will have a real home—but it'll feel so natural and inevitable that it won't seem "designed" at all.

In practical terms, composed relaxation is expressed in the idea of flow, both within a room—how a particular space is organized for use—and between rooms. The latter is particularly important, because as space is reconstructed and new connections are created, wonderful opportunities can be found to get the most out of the square footage—not only in terms of creating additional rooms, but in the ordinarily unused connecting areas between them. Everyone loves a design bargain. And giving the flow-space that joins two rooms its own character and utility makes for an especially rewarding two-for-one, as when a dark and narrow hallway is expanded to become an art gallery, library, or cozy nook.

Maximizing the value of all of the space in an apartment not only results in a richer, more complex environment. It also reinforces one of life's great maxims: The journey is as important as the destination.

While creating virtual rooms requires finding an unseen order in an open space, apartment design involves the same idea in reverse: taking a warren of poorly communicating rooms, strangely shaped hallways, and awkwardly positioned structural elements and transforming it into a suite of clean, well-functioning, harmonious spaces. Not all apartments are so challenging, of course—though they seem to be in New York.

Because I am an architect as well as a designer, it's my experience that taking down walls—creating space, then replacing it with more thoughtfully organized space—produces a better result than trying to hide troublesome architecture behind a layer of decoration. The objective is a feeling of what I call "composed relaxation"—that is, a plan that responds to your personal tastes, in the context of the story you want to tell.

All great cities have "hot zones"—parks or monuments or boulevards to which everyone is almost magnetically drawn—and the same is true of residential interiors. That's what I mean when I say that a space conveys a sense of what it wants to be. At the same time, all of us know how we like to live—the times of day we enjoy light, how and where we prefer to entertain, the rooms that need to feel expansive or cozy. And just as I work to find a story and create order by letting a space speak to me, I encourage my clients to let go of their notions of how they believe they should live and focus on how they truly want to inhabit

Inspiration was derived from sculptor Louise Nevelson, whose large-scale works combine abstraction and asymmetry into mysteriously cohesive narratives.

FIFTH AVENUE ART HOUSE

Keen on a clean environment in which everything extraneous could be put away, the owners of this apartment that looks out across Fifth Avenue to the incomparable vista of Central Park were very specific regarding their desires. The architecture had to provide an almost gallery-like showcase for their extensive sculpture collection. And as people with an appreciation for precious things, the pair wanted each space to be crafted in a distinctive way: to optimize its function, to sharpen its qualities to a fine degree.

Changes to the overall layout were minor. Walls on either side of the entry gallery were removed, creating an unbroken park view from front to back. The gallery, ordinarily an open space, converts to a dining room via the addition of a custom-designed folding table. A former maid's room became an office, and the study doubles as a guest bedroom. Nevertheless, the apartment changed dramatically: the two major interior masonry walls—separating the living room from the master suite and the den from the study—were demolished and replaced with double-sided cabinetry, which we filled to the smallest square inch: art display in the living room; closets, drawers, and a banquette in the bedroom; a media center in the den; and a desk, shelving, and office storage in the study. We infused the rich palette of woods, which included anigre, walnut, oak, and ash, with additional warmth with indirect and cove lighting.

I also designed nearly all of the furnishings, some of which express the rectilinear, puzzlelike quality of the new rooms' design. That quality I derived from a great inspiration: the sculptor Louise Nevelson, whose large-scale works combine abstraction and asymmetry into mysteriously cohesive narratives. Nevelson's influence appears most strongly in the living room art display wall, a collage of slipped boxes and shelves set at different depths and heights and animated by concealed lighting, which began as a freehand drawing and formalized into a sculptural object in its own right.

I'm pleased with my design. But I am prouder of the fact that, once my clients' collection

Walls on either side of the entry were removed, abcve,
creating an unbroken view from the front of the apartment
to the back. A flower-filled vitrine, left, helps to shape space.

In the master suite, a Le Corbusier-inspired chaise,
built into the millwork wall, creates a cozy nook for
contemplating the view of Central Park outside.

MURRAY HILL TOWNHOUSE

In my first years as a designer, my approach favored the monochromatic—rooms were white and related to one another stylistically. But as I worked with greater frequency in New York townhouses, many of which had been expanded over time and combined different architectural styles, I began to wonder: Why not embrace the diversity and organize the variations under a single theme?

That was my approach when a couple asked me to redesign their townhouse duplex. The multiple spaces, dating from the nineteenth century through the 1930s, were of different scales, styles, and even ceiling heights. My clients requested modernity and luxury, which suggested a streamlined plan. But they also wanted each room to have a separate character, for different kinds of social events—a salon for intimate gatherings, a combined art gallery and dining room, and so forth. My solution was to harmonize these seemingly opposite desires: simplifying the spaces and the relationships between them, while also giving each room a distinct personality.

On the first floor, I removed walls from the entry area to create a grand dining and gallery space, and widened and straightened a circuitous hallway; upstairs, I added a bath and powder room, and combined two bedrooms into a salon. Whenever possible I try to make connecting spaces part of the larger living experience, and reorganizing the first-floor hallway afforded the chance to turn what had been a transitional zone into a display area for a collection of Chinese ceramics.

The design of the individual rooms evolved, in most instances, from their existing qualities. The family room's beamed ceiling and dark floors inspired a gun-metal mantelpiece and a custom-designed sideboard, its dark English oak pierced by illuminated apertures. Directly above it, the master bedroom, with its extra-high ceilings and nineteenth-century details, suggested a classically romantic treatment, which we answered with an ornate English limestone fireplace, a Venetian mirror, and a French mirrored secretary.

The design of the salon, conversely, was dictated by an object—my clients' Empire settee—that posed an interesting challenge. I would never have selected the piece. But as with the architecture's diversity, I chose to embrace it: making it the room's centerpiece, surrounding the settee with contrastingly modern but no less authoritative furnishings, and dramatizing its gold leaf and white upholstery with a backdrop of oxblood curtains. If you've inherited some outlandish object from Grandma and can't imagine how to make it work, this is definitely the way to go.

What had been a dark and narrow corridor was expanded and redesigned, above, to create a gallery for the display of the owners' collection of Chinese ceramics. The gallery flows naturally into the sitting room at right—at once connected to and separate from it.

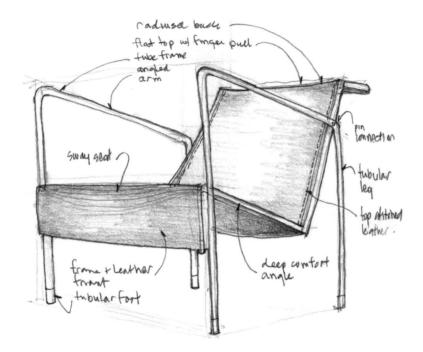

radiused back
flat top w/ finger pull
tube frame
angled
arm

sway seat

pin
connection

tubular
leg

top stitched
leather.

frame + leather
front
tubular foot

deep comfort
angle

Contemporary canvas-and-steel chairs were custom-designed
to match the authority of the residents' oversized Empire settee.
The effect in the sitting room is like a grouping of generals—
some young, some old, all proudly displaying their stars.

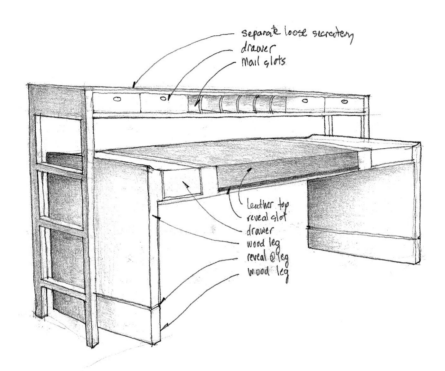

separate loose secretary
drawer
Mail slots

Leather top
reveal slot
drawer
wood leg
reveal @ leg
wood leg

The custom desk at right, which combines a generous
work surface with a separate hopper for accessories, is
an instant classic—both for the design and for the care
and elegance with which the cabinetmaker executed it.

Since the dining room, above, was meant to double as a gallery space, a custom sculptural table with an organic French aspen top and a nickel base—a truly artisanal piece—was created to reinforce the theme. In a room in an older part of the apartment, right, a bold gun-metal mantelpiece echoes the heavy beaming of the preexisting ceiling.

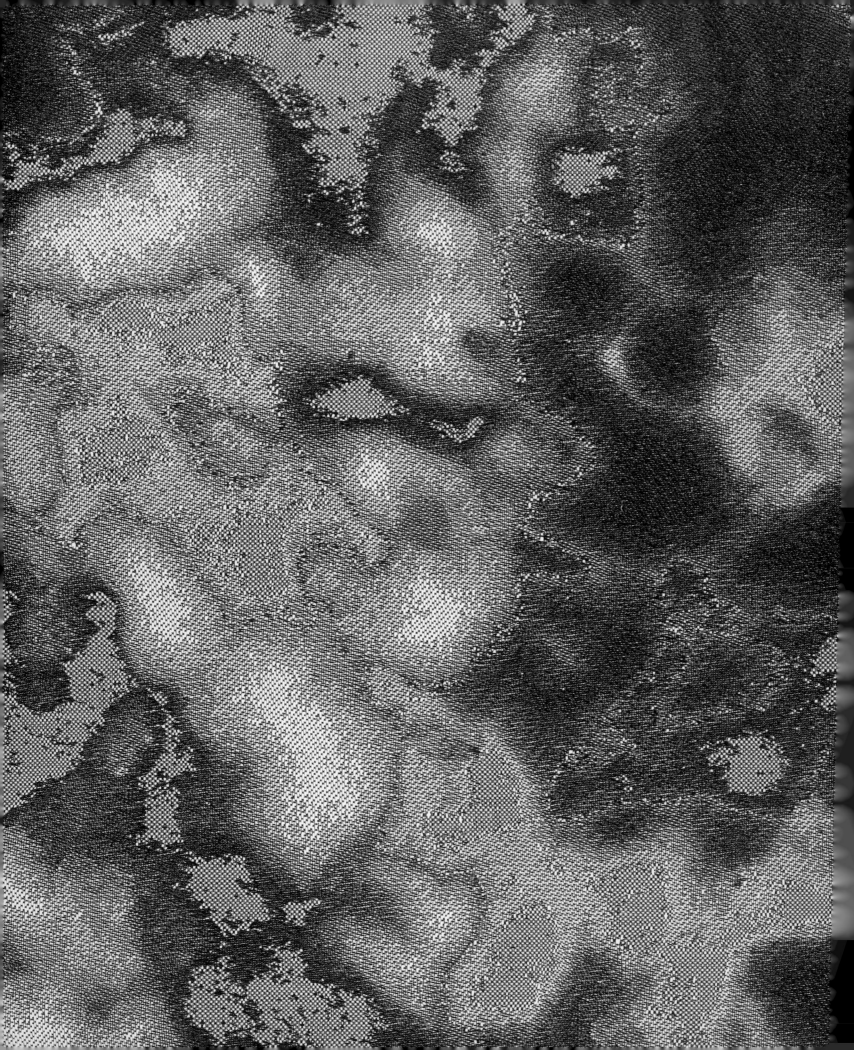

CONTRASTS

Most people remain susceptible to the idea of the "camera-ready" showplace room, in which every element has been selected and arranged to match perfectly with everything else, and nothing has been left to chance. The problem with such spaces is that no one ever wants to go into them. Remember your parents' formal living room, in which you weren't allowed to touch anything, the room that was only used on holidays and "important" occasions? It was designed not for people, but to make a statement—and as such felt not only unwelcoming, but rather depressingly embalmed.

What's missing from these spaces is tension—not the nervous-making sort, but the kind of visual and spatial drama that can vitalize a room out of a state of complacency. One of the surest ways to achieve this is by creating contrasts: between thick and thin, restriction and freedom, symmetry and asymmetry, the historic and the contemporary. The more a design can confound expectation—and do so with style, sophistication, and a sense of fun—the more welcoming it will prove to be.

Sometimes this can be achieved by placing a thin, elegantly designed lamp in proximity to a thick and blocky coffee table, producing a kind of electric charge between them. Or I may choose to layer the furnishings or structural elements within a room to create moments of compression and release—much as Frank Lloyd Wright, one of my great inspirations, would design a low-ceilinged entry hall before letting a space explode gloriously upward. Rather than laying out a symmetrical furniture plan, I'll occasionally use objects to shape a circulation route that meanders with the pleasurable sense of surprise one finds in an English garden, or else create what I call a "canyon" effect, building elements gradually upward and backward from a void at the center of a room to the walls (the last step perhaps being a tall folding screen).

I often work in prewar apartment buildings or historic homes, and instead of completely modernizing them or engaging in architectural preservation, I'll mediate between the two, creating a dialogue between past and present in which each amplifies the other. This can be practiced in the decoration as well, by combining sleekly machined modern design pieces with craft objects or handmade fabrics and wall coverings. And though a project may have a strongly stated story, it's sometimes possible to tell a number of different but related tales moving from room to room—in effect, playing variations on a theme.

The more I work, the more I recognize that the possibilities for creating contrasts—many of which have been suggested by my clients—are limited only by the willingness to keep imagining them. The pleasures they produce are equal to those of meeting new people: there's invariably a surprise, and it's frequently enriching.

HUDSON VALLEY PASTORAL

How does a designer create interiors for a historic house that are apparently of the period, yet still possess a contemporary flavor? That was the dilemma posed by this private estate, located on 125 magnificent Hudson Valley acres near West Point. Though the residence was completed recently, the design—with its layers of columned terraces, axial plan, and generously proportioned spaces—harkens back to the elegant country manors of the Gilded Age. My clients, great lovers of Americana, had sought precisely that spirit with their choice of style. But they wanted to live in the present—reminding me that their children would be running in and out in their muddy boots—and asked me to inject a modern informality and freshness without undermining the "historic" story.

Certain of my decisions informed the design direction of the structure. The house has no formal living room, but rather a generous space combining a highly functional kitchen and more relaxed family room; in collaboration with the architect, Ralph Mackin, we enclosed the kitchen in a pavilion, with a half-wall, columns, and transom windows, to separate it from, but also communicate with, the living room. Elsewhere we developed a tension between old and new: increasing the dining room's formality with a massive corner cabinet to balance the fireplace opposite it, while enlivening the walls with a robin's-egg blue Venetian plaster; contrasting the finely detailed woodwork of the family room fireplace with a fascia of roughly textured brick.

The house features a number of important eighteenth- and nineteenth-century Hudson Valley artworks and antiques, and our bespoke furnishings had to pass what I call the "squint test": if you walk into a room and squint your eyes, all the pieces should harmonize—but when you open them and look closely, the new work reveals its quirky, personal quality. So the classic highboy in the master suite turns out to be finished in tambour, a material ordinarily reserved for sliding panels, and the library's Mission-style Morris chair proves, on closer inspection, to have an exposed wood frame that recalls Le Corbusier's early modernist designs. Upholstered sofas and settees in the family room present more streamlined profiles, and are more loosely tailored than their historic predecessors to suit a contemporary lifestyle.

One custom piece—the smallest—says it all: a simple wooden Flag Side Chair, its tractor seat supported by dowelled legs, and backrest pierced by random "American flag" stars— but with a profile reminiscent of Arne Jacobsen's Danish modern Ant Chair. It's a classic tale, told in the language of our time.

A panoramic vista of the Hudson River, above. The dayroom, right, is furnished with an interpretation of the overstuffed sofas and chairs that were popular at the turn of the last century—just as comfortable, but with cleaner lines and softer tailoring.

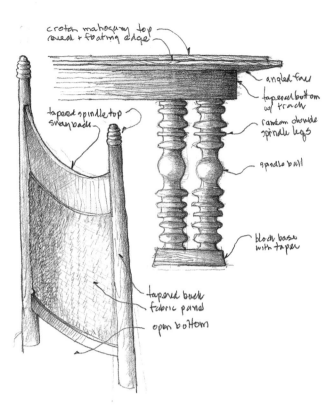

croton mahogany top
reveal + floating edge!

angled face

tapered bottom w/ track

random diameter spindle legs

spindle ball

block base with taper

tapered spindle top swayback

tapered back fabric panel

open bottom

Ricardo Brizola's robin's-egg blue Venetian plaster walls lighten and contemporize the house's most formal room, below and opposite. Surrounded by antique pieces, the custom table and chairs are sufficiently vernacular in style to fit in. The table's long span, however, was only made possible by steel reinforcements, which were not available a century ago when most of the room's other furnishings were created.

CARNEGIE HILL ZEN

This penthouse duplex on Carnegie Hill is home to a couple with young children who had just moved back from Asia, and wanted to preserve the traditional qualities of their home—the richness of material and refined craftwork—while adjusting them to suit the demands of modern-day New York life. I took a twofold approach: opening up the plan and eliminating rooms that had outlived their historic use, like the separate pantry; and creating details that, while speaking a modern language, remained classically based—and no less luxurious—than those enjoyed by the families who had resided there in generations past.

On the lower floor, the twin entrances to the living room from the foyer were enlarged, the outmoded pantry eliminated to make way for a more grand but flexible dining space—the perfect setting for an elegant dinner party—and the maid's room turned into a relaxed sitting area and an informal home office. Upstairs, in addition to restyling the relatively modest bedrooms, we created what I named the "Manhattan library," for the way in which the bookshelves and cabinets step back as they ascend, mimicking the setbacks of the city's skyscrapers.

Our detail work took two forms. The apartment's inner core reveals the kind of custom cabinetry and craftwork associated with old-line Carnegie Hill luxury, notably the main stair, which with its built-in storage and patterned design tips its hat to the Craftsman style. In the lighter, more formal outer ring of rooms overlooking the wraparound terrace and panoramic views, the focus is on the moldings. These recall the robustness of the past, but float off the ceilings, giving them a lighter, more modern expression—all calibrated to pass my "squint test."

This contrast between inner and outer spaces serves various purposes. It strengthens the distinction between the residence's dark and light zones. It relieves the public rooms of the burdens of storage and allows them to be about the pleasures of light, space, and views. And—given the power of first impressions—greeting visitors with handsome millwork, beautiful woods, and custom craftsmanship establishes a tone of manorial elegance in the clouds.

The owners of this duplex brought many of
their furnishings with them from Asia, where
they had lived previously. Though the furniture
is Eastern, its formal elegance suits a Western
living room that is similar in mood.

Combining the original kitchen and large service pantry, which had become functionally outmoded, allowed creation of a breakfast area, space for a cooking island, and a lounge/play area for entertaining children and guests while cooking.

A wall-size world map in a child's room, right, captures the family's international spirit. Though the clients are both American-born, they chose to preserve the Asian decorative style and material palette with which they had fallen in love. Accordingly, the walls of their bedroom are finished in white silk, above, and the master bath, opposite, features jade green marble.

HIGHRISE REDUX

While everyone wants a large apartment, it's my experience that how spacious a place seems to be actually matters more than how substantial it truly is. One of the strongest arbiters of this is what I characterize as the "threshold factor": what confronts you—or, rather, doesn't confront you—upon stepping through the main entrance. Thus I try to create a long view from the front door, ideally a steadily widening sightline that culminates in a window with a view. No matter how small the space, an unobstructed vista invariably produces a welcome sense of volume and connects enclosed space to the out of doors.

In this three-bedroom New York apartment, the original layout presented a wall opposite the front door, after which a mazelike hallway led to a narrow living room. The residence wasn't small, but following this introduction—which terminated in a compressed space—it seemed so, despite the living room's floor-to-ceiling windows.

My solution was to remove enough of the hallway and living room walls—in effect, cutting away a large L-shaped piece of structure—to open a view from the front door directly to the living room's curtain wall: immediately upon entry, some 60 feet away, awaited the muscular Manhattan cityscape. Following that simple move, the apartment felt enormous; we enhanced the experience by removing the remainder of the living room wall and replacing it with a double-sided millwork volume that lightly divides the main living space from the adjacent guest room—which was recast as a den—and makes both feel like related areas of a loft.

Another example of spatial sleight of hand turns up in the master bedroom. To create more storage, I crafted a wall of cabinets, incorporating a vanity, which subtracted 18 inches from the floor plan. At the same time, we placed a wall-size upholstered headboard behind the bed, installing vertical light coves on either side, to make it seem as though the entire panel is floating. Doing so creates a layer that suggests the room is deeper—so what I took away in actuality I returned psychologically.

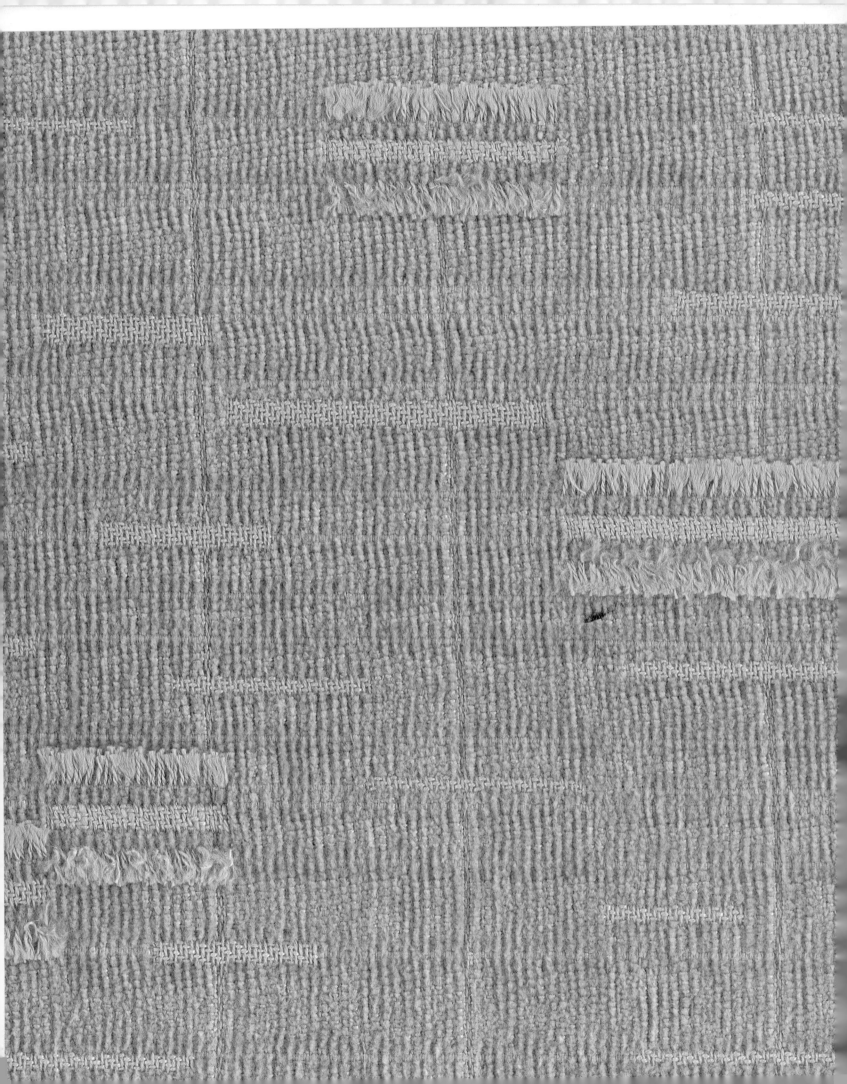

NATURE AND CRAFT

SKY LOUNGE

When I first saw this space, it struck me as the ultimate example of a certain kind of hard-edged New York apartment: forty stories above Manhattan, the towers of Midtown looming just beyond the floor-to-ceiling glass. How does a designer bring nature into an environment so aggressively urban?

I worked from the ground up. Just beyond the foyer, we embedded Japanese river rocks in a wide band of concrete running the full width of the public rooms; beyond it, we set marquetry "leaves" into the maple floor. A visitor enters and, after figuratively washing off the urban grit in the stream's cleansing waters, arrives in the forest with its spare carpet of fallen foliage.

The "forest" itself I constructed from layers of wood, glass, and furniture. A five-panel accordion metal-and-glass door opens the living room to the den; a double-sided millwork wall separates the den from the bedroom. Custom furnishings are overtly organic: the wooden dining tabletop sits on razor-thin steel panels that recall shark fins; the tiered glass coffee table supports resemble rough-cut stone; a tulip-shaped chair blooms on the edge of the living room; slabs and stacks of gray maple form a desk in the den. A vitrine of orchids also conceals one of the massive structural piers.

Yet it's impossible in such a setting to ignore the presence of the city—indeed, who would want to?—and so we also found ways of drawing it in. The tubular metal frames of some furnishings echo the window mullions, which themselves restate the urban grid beyond the glass. A standing screen with a built-in lightbox, constructed to conceal a support pier, captures the shape of the surrounding skyscrapers. To me, one of the bonuses of an environment this exposed is that the view effectively becomes part of the apartment; to help my client enter it, I set a long, underlit vitrine containing five thousand clear glass marbles at a point where the floor meets the curtain wall, to erase the connection between them.

The outcome is an intricately layered intermingling of the urban and organic. It's an oasis of natural calm amid passing helicopters and expanses of tinted glass.

A translucent glass wall, which brings light into the apartment's interior while providing privacy, can be completely folded away to unite the guest bedroom/office with the living room.

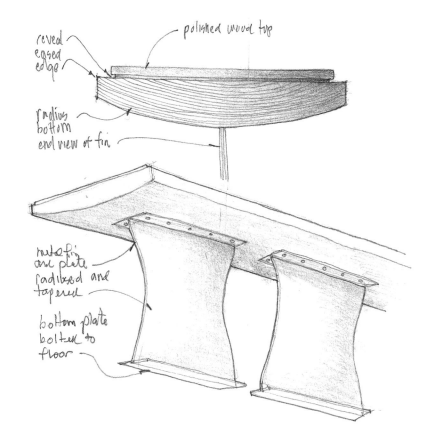

polished wood top

reveal
eased
edge

radius
bottom
end view of fin

note fin
and plate
radiused and
tapered

bottom plate
bolted to
floor

Custom furnishings—including the dining table, which features razor-thin supports resembling shark fins, and a tulip-shaped chair—are frankly organic in character.

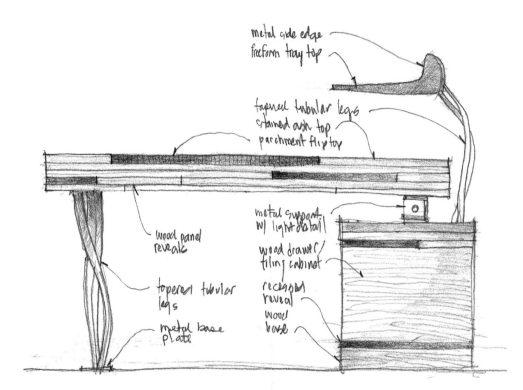

metal side edge
freeform tray top

tapered tubular legs
stained ash top
parchment flip top

metal support
w/ light detail

wood panel
reveals

wood drawer/
filing cabinet

tapered tubular
legs

recessed
reveal
wood
base

metal base
plate

The design of this desk, which has the appearance of stacked
lumber, is echoed in the lighting fixture directly above it—the boards
are pulled apart to reveal and release the illumination within.

In the master suite, right,
cabinetry provides material
warmth and visual complexity.
The powder room, opposite,
reflects a window view.

craft into architecture, as with my Eiffel Tower table and a desk that drew on the form of the main terminal at New York's LaGuardia Airport. But these iconic, contrasting pieces were telling the same story as the others, so rather than seeming out of place, they played in harmony.

This Long Island home was envisioned as a hunting lodge that had "gone designer." Found materials became many of the fixtures and furnishings, such as the fireplace's log holder and the wood rails that serve as curtain rods.

The piece above, named the LaGuardia Desk, borrows its
design from the main terminal at one of New York's airports.
In the dining room, opposite, a rope-wrapped table is paired
with bentwood chairs made from knotty pine—with the knots
removed to create an intriguing decorative array of holes.

A custom-designed chest, above, is paired with a George Nelson chaise. No animals were harmed in the making of the billiard room chandelier, opposite. The antlers were found and gathered by the Boy Scouts of America.

A dresser covered in raffia,
right, reinforces the rustic
mood of the master suite. The
base of the ironwork table
drew upon the structure of the
Eiffel Tower, opposite.

This outdoor room, which has a glass ceiling above the latticework and is enclosed on both sides, is sufficiently sheltered to be used in all but the coldest months.

CITY HUES

This commission proved atypical in several respects. The brief was to design two side-by-side apartments on the thirtieth floor of a building in Manhattan, which would tell different versions of the same story. The client, a Tucson-based spa, was opening a New York City outpost and combining it with a residential component. My task involved creating interiors that would express the essence of Upper East Side elegance, imbued with an organic component of total wellness.

Essential to both ideas was making the public rooms of each apartment feel expansively proportioned—which was difficult, since their layouts were in fact confining. Certain solutions were obvious, such as combining the third bedroom of the larger unit with the living room into a grand space. But I was also able to make the apartments feel bigger via the use of millwork elements, which created a contrast with the surrounding painted walls, too. Into the expanded living room of what had been the three-bedroom residence, I inserted a burl-wood-wrapped volume that combined closets, bookshelves, and a media center; each of its four sides, which effectively formed the face of a different room, helped to define a separate and distinct zone—something that can be economically achieved, by non-professionals, with colors or wallpaper. In the smaller apartment's living room, I added a chocolate-colored wenge wood cabinet that began as a counter beneath the living room window, turned a corner and flowed down the room's long wall, then turned another corner and disappeared down a hallway—stretching to connect the residence's darkest reaches to the expansive, sunlit view.

Color, texture, and the use of organic materials also contributed to the designs' effectiveness. To create a sense of repose, each apartment expressed the idea of a transplanted spa experience with a different color scheme: the larger mixed the gray tones of a southwestern dusk with a more urban-industrial indigo; the smaller captured the orange clay of a desert mesa in the sofa upholstery and living room lamps. In one residence, an irregularly shaped slab of walnut serves as a dining table. And textured walls—gridded, ribbed, dense with pigment—infuse different rooms in both apartments with warmth and tactility.

This last was crucial. I always believe that a home should be an oasis; in these organic environments—after a day spent trying to keep your hands off the urban grime—everything was delightfully, invitingly touchable.

Multiple textured surfaces and strongly graphic artwork and objects help to enliven this Manhattan apartment. The approach: light, fresh, new, modern.

In the smaller of the two apartments, the orange clay of a southwestern desert mesa was expressed in the color of the sofa and lamps. A chocolate-colored wenge wood cabinet, opposite, begins as a counter beneath the living room window.

The warmth of the apartments' interiors, and their Zenlike calm, stand in contrast to the dynamic urban condition that surrounds them.

With a few simple gestures, a room that could only accommodate two functions was transformed into a room that could accommodate six.

Into a preexisting niche at the living room's rear, above and opposite, a custom-designed banquette and table create a new dining area.

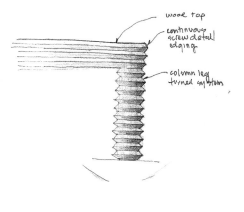

wood top

continuous screw detail edging

column leg turned custom

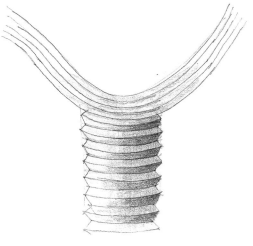

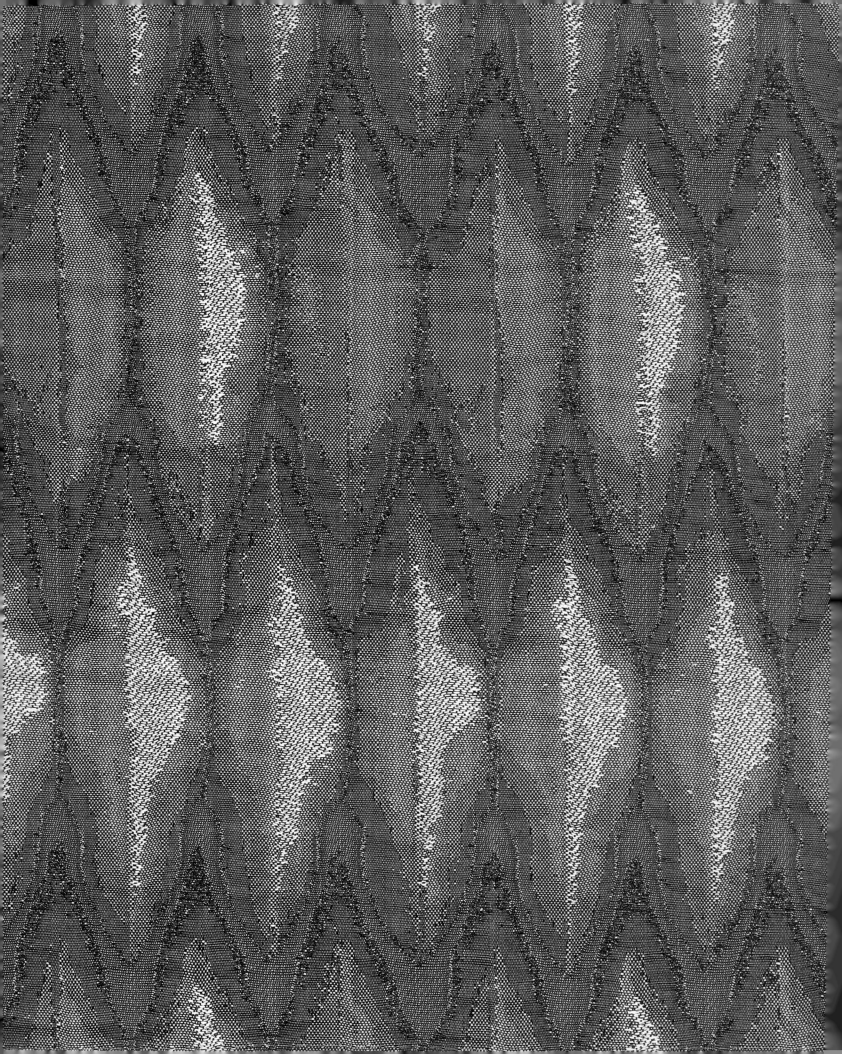

SOLUTIONS

As dinner would always be a candlelit affair in this apartment, a piece of art—in this case, a mobile—is suspended over the table in lieu of a lamp, right and opposite. A glamorous dark floor unifies the room's various functions and reflects light by day and by night.

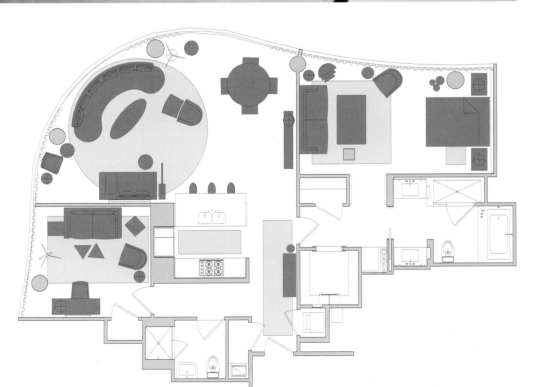

In the guest room/office, above and right—the most predictably
shaped of the apartment's spaces—the chocolate-colored

A contemplative corner in the bedroom serves as a second
writing space, above. A porous shelving unit, opposite,
cleverly screens the apartment's home office from the living
room, and makes the overall space seem larger. Four
three-sided glass vitrines enclose sculptural objects.

For my loving and always supportive wife, my amore, Tatiana,
Jeremy, and my new little ones Fox and Xenia.

ACKNOWLEDGMENTS

Genius creates sparks for the truly inspired, collaborations fulfill the dream. I have always preached that our design work and the resulting homes for our clients are only as good as the first perception on which we deliver. As I revisited all the designs in this book, I reflected on the clients, the process, and all the superbly custom-crafted details, and what I remembered most were the wonderful teams I worked with in the creation of these interiors. Each project had its special circumstances which allowed for unique solutions. In the spirit of a true team, each architect and designer in the studio contributed heavily to the process. In our world of "made to order" design, the details are what shine most for our clients.

There could be no custom work without input of the many great artisans with whom I have collaborated. I would like to give special thanks to Chris Tekvert, Mike Arruda, Thomas Tommi, Frank Caramanica, Robert Linker, Emily Nomer, Barbara Fiore, Marylee Egusquiza and especially my friend and master Venetian plaster artisan, Ricardo Brizola. And I hope you enjoyed the many images by my friend and photographer Scott Frances.

In addition to all my great staff, I must acknowledge Paige Rense, Editor in Chief of *Architectural Digest* for her ardent support of my many "bespoke" designs. Paige has watched my evolving style and has been there supporting it each time.

A word about Jay McInerney, who wrote the foreword. A longtime friend and design supporter, Jay embodies the ideal client. Jay trusted me implicitly with few comments and was always happily surprised at each unique solution. Friendship goes a long way, but design must inspire to be great and really appreciated.

In this spirit, I am grateful as well for the positive responses I have had from my very generous clients. I remember one who called me on the eve of his move-in to say that his wife was crying in the kitchen. Oh, no! I thought. Was there a leak, something broken, an uncomfortable sofa? As it turned out, she was crying because she loved the design—it had far exceeded her expectations.

Finally, a very special thank-you to the people who made this book possible: My inexhaustible agent Jill Cohen, who worked hard to find it a home; my perceptive, patient editors Andrea Monfried, Elizabeth White, and Stacee Lawrence; and in particular my publisher Gianfranco Monacelli, who in some ways understood my work better than I did.

And remember: If your design inspiration is based on a good story, your interiors will truly have a soul.

STAFF 1990-PRESENT

Adrian Williams

Adrienne Broadbear

Alberto Blanquel

Alex Wilbur

Alice Cho

Alicia Taylor

Amelie Chai

Amy Muir

Andrea China Morgan

Anubha Singh

Barbara Fiore

Beatriz Cal

Berns Fry

Blanca Rivera

Chad Firmstone

Chris Tekverk

Christine Carroll

Christopher Howe

Christopher Rinaldi

Constanza Collarte

Dalit Acosta

Damian Petrescu

Daniel Wismer

Darlene Marone

Darryl Cook

David Nath

Dorn Rice

Elyasse Benmekki

Emily Aund-Din

Emily Fischer

Emily Nomer

Eric Hilton

Eunice Kim

Evan Chi-Man Chan

Frank Caramanica

Georgi Petrov

Gloria Herrera

Greta Hansen

Guss Firestein

Heagyeong Kweon

Heather Johnston

Heather Moore

Heather Mosher

Hye Jin Lim

Itaru Yanagawa

Jackie Franco

Jaime Gutierrez

Janne Neglia

Jennifer Jeffery

Jeremy Platt

Jim Hanson

Jonovic Krunica

Julie Chia-Ping

Justin Onicar

Katherine Starr Law

Katie Crider

Katy Hines

Kavitha Mathew

Keena Suh

Kei Moon

Kelly L. Sung

Kelly Ottinger

Kendall Simmons Kaelin

Kristen Munro

Kyung Soo Lee

Lanna Semel

Lauren Rasmussen

Leslie Hoerig

Lindsey Pate

Lionel Real de Azua

Lorraine Wall

Louis Monaco

Mao-Jung Lee

Mark Tufaro

Mary Arch

Marylee Egusquiza

Matthew Barlow

Maya Bendgi

Mike Arruda

Michael Waiman

Mimi Betancourt

Min Yoo

Nick Jordache

Nicole Turner

Oren Sagiv

Paul Eltz

Peiheng Tsai

Peter Case

Peter Hilligoss

Ralph Habbel

Rebecca Barron

Rebecca Leesman

Rebecca McKeown

Ricardo Brizolo

Rima Yamamura

Rob Flaws

Robert Linker

Robert Timm

Saaya Yasuda

Sandra McGowan

Sarah Clapper

Sarah Glazer

Sasha Lanka

Sashy Bagdanovich

Scott Hirshson

Seema Shah-Nelson

Shachar Habub

Shay Zurmin

Shirley Leong

Sofia Ames Leak

Ta-Chiun Chou

Tali Midian

Thomas Loftus

Thomas Tommi

Tracy I-Wen Lee

Trisha Elliott

Vanessa Spielman

Willow Ayers

Yael Sahar

Young Hee Jo